The Erotic Café

Words by Ray Hollingsworth
Design by Lee Thomas

© Kiss Production Limited 1999

www.erotic-cafe.net

Reprint 2002

D1283704

ISBN 0 9536958 0 8
Printed by Jenner (City Print) Ltd

Thank you
Robbie Williams
for 'Angels'

Published by Kiss Production

quick nurse

lilac riot

karen and liam

manchester

fuckin 'borin'

the kiss

voice over

nature of the beast

tuesday morning

everything

danger

single mums

dream

a kind of life

10th dimension

channel four

peach

m & s checkout girl

a seaside town in england

nothing

direct marketing

god save the queen

moment

multi coloured army

st john's wood

prostitutes

superdrug

attitude

b & q landscape

yhcnuar ettessac lrig

eastern princess

nightclub girl

hot wire

the emptiness of the day after

small ads

mobile phone girl

hush

quick

nurse

i've just had a baby

get her a nose stud

make her hair u^{n}tid$_y$

bring her a bottle

of diamond white

quick nurse

o deal

show her the dummies

she'll meet at night

and when she's hungry

give her junk food

and when she's angry

give her attitude

make her a clone

just like the rest

get her stoned

when she's depressed

teach her to r   u   n

before she can walk

quick

quick nurse
give her junk food

and when she's a

tell her

teach her to swear

before she can talk

teach her to beg

teach her to steal

show her the way

tell her the deal

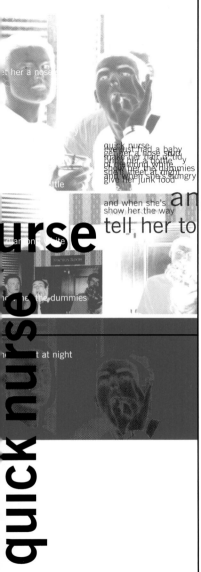

et her a nose

quick nurse
get her a noise a baby
make her a solid
bring her a bottle
of diamond white
show her the dummies
and when she's angry
give her junk food

and when she's angry
show her the way
tell her to deal

urse

ottle

the dummies

st at night

quick nurse

lilac

1

I saw them

in birmingham

in a garage

esso I think

buying coca cola

at midnight

no more

than fourteen

black hair

shiny black hair

and high heels

and I noticed

they both had

the same colour

varnish on

their toenails....

...lilac

they met

at the istanbul kebab

at 2am in romford

she a slimline tonic

with flashing eyes

gleaming nose stud

and tattooed rose bud

on her shoulder

he the silent type

magazine heartthrob

a baywatch pleasuregod

subject of her fantasy

such was the power

of attraction   ·

that suddenly

they found themselves sitting

at the same green plastic table

he with 3 pieces of chicken

karen and liam

and chips

she with a hint

of mayonnaise on her lips

sipping black coffee

outside police cars screamed

they were oblivious

inside the ultimate dream

they were delirious

he liam **karen and liam**

a roof tiler by day

she karen

a chancery lane p.a.

they shook hands

he from a broken home

she who lived alone

they held hands

he 25 in may

she 21 in two days

they kissed

in the background

a crackly def leppard

sung 'all I want is everything'

karen and liam

are engaged to be

married

DIVERSION

r Manchester
r Manchester
r Manchester
r Manchester

m a
n

Manchester

Manchester

Manchester Manchester Manchester
Manchester Manches
Manchester Manches
Manchester Manches
Manch

Manchester Manchester
Manchester Manchester

Manchester Manchester Manchester Manchester Manchester Manche
Manchester Manchester Manchester Manchester Manche.
nchester Manchester Manchester Manchester Manchester Manches

Manchester Manchester Manchester Manchester Manchester ManchesterManches
Manchester Manchester Manchester Manchester ManchesterManchester Manchester Manchester Manchester Manchester Manche

Manchester

Manchester   Manchester

Manchester

Manchester

Manchester   Manchester   Manchester   Manch

your star in the distance

lights up the

h   o   r   i   z   o   n

your very being is intoxicating the landscape

picking up your signal

which is **stronger** than ever

i head off the motorway

and into your

air s   p   a   c   e

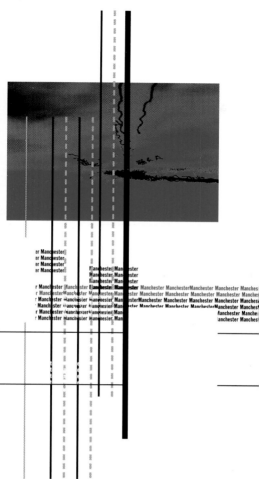

in a thousand lifetimes i never knew this

the sound of your doorbell

sends shivers right through me

your shape in the hallway

moves closer and closer

now in your presence

hopelessly addicted

laying beside you is this a dream

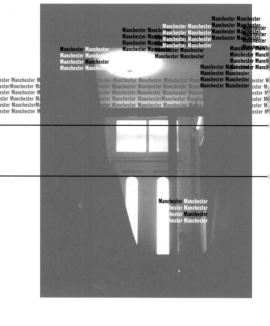

one day when this is all over

i will thank god for the life that he

gave me.

I think tony's

gone off sex

either that

or'es gettin' it

somewhere else

seems more interested

in the bloody internet

or'es music lessons

with es' clarinet

sometimes I feel

like stuffin the fing

up 'es arse

can't remember

the last time

we'ad a good laugh

or the last time

we kissed...

...oh yeah

it was at e's bruvvers

when they got pissed

fuckin' borin' fuckin' borin' fuckin' fuc

I dressed up for im

the other week

in me anne summers gear

but'e went to sleep

e' didn't come near

to think there was a time

e' couldn't get enough

we'd only just met

an' I was up the duff

god e's so
fuckin borin!

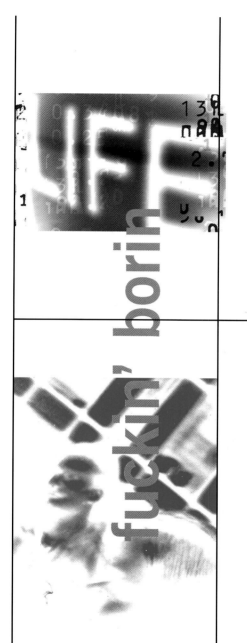

fuckin' borin

...and so

after a few

phone calls

they decided

to meet

secretly

by nightfall

in a dimly

lit street

her children

sleeping

in their beds

her husband

believing

what she'd said

in fourteen years

she always

been true

but how she

yearned

for something new

as she drove

her mind was racing

her hand was shaking

at the wheel

a tingling excitement

she did feel...

would they touch

would they kiss

would it all be

worth

the risk...

the
kiss

the morning after

in her kitchen

sipping coffee

and reliving

every moment...

we
apologise
for
the
delay **v o i c e**
in
your
service
tonight
this
is
entirely
due
to
the
north
fifteen
moon
light

so
lay
down
on
the
cool
kitchen
floor
talk
to
the
pop
stars
on
the
fridgerator
door

count
very
slowly
from
one
to
a
thousand
gaze
up
at
the
ceiling
phase
out
every
feeling
read
the
text
on
the

soap
box
that
says
for   **o   v   e   r**
superb
results
we
recommend
comfort   then
then   two
ask   weeks
yourself   later
what   on
do   an
they   escalator
know   in
as   a
you   west
breathe   end
in   store
the   you
soap   see
suds   a
and   face
bask   in
in   a
the   space
glory   on
of   a   put
the   cool   her
after   ceramic   back
flow   floor   in
                 pick   the
                 her   folder
                 up   that
                 and   she
                                      slipped
                                      from
                                      the
                                      one
                                      labelled
                                      'the
                                      ultimate
                                      collection'

**such is
the nature of the beast**
that occasionally
she needs to be
released
from the confines of
her kids to school
shopping drool mornings

or her
washing machine
keep the house clean
afternoons
of her
zero love action
passionless nights

where sometimes
she awakes at 3am
and looks beside her
at the man
she no longer loves

nature of the beast

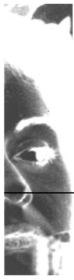

such is
the nature of the beast
commonly known
as housewife
society's acceptable
low life
soon to be
an endangered species
suffering from
a universal disease
called boredom

and how she longs
for those
business trip nights
when he is away
and she can play
with fire
into the pleasuredome
where danger dances
with desire

such is
the nature of the beast
who hunts down
her prey
with an all action display
of enticing walk
and body talk
with predatory instinct
she closes in
and corners him
her object of desire

nature of the beast

two cigarettes later
they dance and touch
in this modern form
of manufactured love
which is
as instant as a
scratchcard

last dance at 2am
french kiss
she leaves with him
such is the nature of....

surreal dreams

erotic scenes

in a laundrette

where you

lost the thread

over the border

no law

no order

the fantasy

that fills

your head

tu

da

tues-day morn-ing

misty morning

princess

you've really
done it
this time

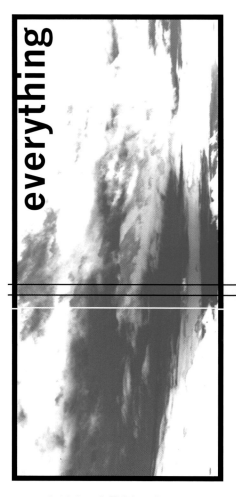

everything

YOU ARE 1st
IN THE QUEUE

114

8:06:28pm   16/11 1998

'tis the dawn
of a new day
as the lovelorn
drift away
from places
where they stray
in pursuit of...

'tis the
never ending search
the wonder of the words
the hunger
and the thirst
in pursuit of...

'tis the
burning desire
the flame
that lights the fire
a plane
that takes you higher
the very root of...

everything

everything

Do not
lean out of
the windows

Do not
lean on or open the doors
when the building
is moving

If the doors
are not properly closed
and the building
is moving
do not attempt to
close them
use the emergency
alarm to alert
the driver

Have a nice day

DANGER

amazing really

the young mums

down at the school

chewing gum

the new age modules

most of them

on benefits they say

no sign of the dads

that went astray

which in some way

goes to explain

why they're like it

amazing really

how they survive

to many others

they seem deprived

but somehow

they get by

and what's more

occasionally

they explore

the finer things

in life

amazing really

the transformation

on wednesday nights

synchronised

gyration

in disco lights

respite from

the incubation

of modern life

a place where

they can put

their world

to right

which

in some way...

single mums

Dream

heavenly

whispers

in

the

still

of

night

tender

the

touch

by

naked

moon

light

drift

into

dreams

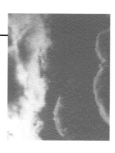

i

dreameth

of

you

tis

here

that

you

breathe

the

dream

cometh

true

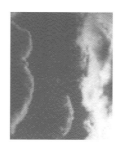

a kind of life

happy shopper baked beans

tabloids and nicotian

council flats of b ro k e   n   dreams

adolescents sniffing glue

anti-depressants and benefit q
                             u
                             e
                             u
                             e
six figure salaries   s

for the chosen few

a kind of life

Put on

that slinky

black dress

that clings

to the contours

of your

incredible

body

put on

your diamond

earrings

that reflect

starlight

on all that

come near you

put on

the high heels

you bought

in milan

whose echoes

are heard

by gods in

the heavens

shake your hair

let it fall

on your shoulders

making you look

lovelier

than ever

spray

on the fragrance

that makes

you white hot

and takes

you into the

tenth dimension

give me a drug

that numbs

the senses

for I am

in danger

of drowning

in your ocean

10th
dime
nsio
n

your spaceship

landed

on a saturday

I planned

a cosy

night just

the cat and me

I was

watching

the news

on channel four

your

five foot three halo

appeared

at the door

your floor show

took me

by surprise

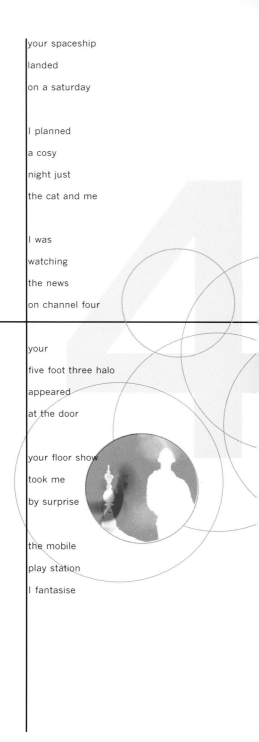

the mobile

play station

I fantasise

and you

promised

to stay

the night

if I

fed you

chocolate

biscuits

by

candlelight.

channel four

mummy daddy

I want you
to buy me
a peach for my
birthday

I want
a real one
not one
from a tin

I want to
feel one

I want
the real thing

I want
to run my fingers
over the texture
of its skin

I want to feel

its juices

r u n n i n g

d

o

w

n

my chin

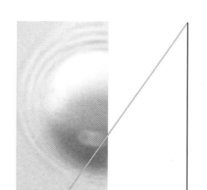

SIZE: **XL**

peach

m&s checkout girl

she is
100% natural
as nature intended
only top quality fruit
for best flavour
the ultimate in freshness
squeezed and packed
within 24 hours
keep her refrigerated
shake her well before consuming

typical value: 100% energy
fat trace: very little
serving suggestion: as often as
possible

made in the u.k.
for marks and spencer p.l.c.

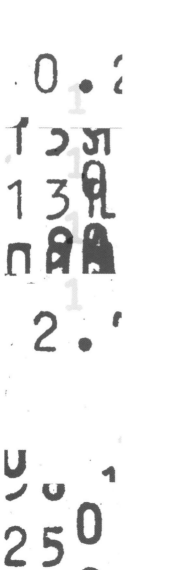

super market trollies blue rinse mollies
barbie dollies love top man wallies

a seaside town in England

single mums chewing gum plastic guns and
real ones

a sea
side
town
in
Engla n
d

wish I
wasn't
here

essex ten fifteen

college boy dreams

of college girl....

...rep gains entry

via video comm

to gaze upon

secretary

on swivel chair

with revlon

system hair

and dream on

underwear...

nothing

clonesclonesclonesclonesclonesclocloclones

...2 miles away

toddlers play

near kids

in bomber jackets

exchanging

secret packets

while avon van

arrives

with supplies

of pretty eyes

to brighten

up the lives

of abandoned

lonely wives...

nothin
g

nothing

clonesclonesclonesclonesclonesclo-
clonesclonesclonesclonesclo
nesclonesclonesclon
esclonesclonesclonesclonesclo
nesclonesclonesclonesclonescl
onesclonesclonesclonesclonesc
lonesclonesclonesclonesclones
clonesclonesclonesclonesclone
sclonesclonesclonesclonesclon
esclonesnes

...meanwhile

back in town

mobile clones

from bovis homes

stalk the street

and arrange to meet

top man labels

at sugar cube

tables

to talk about...

....nothing

nothing

nothing

clonesclonesclonesclonesclonescloclonesclo
nesclonesclonesclo
nesclonesclonesclonesclonesclonesclonesc
lonesclonesclonsclonesclonesclonesclones
clonesclones nesclonescl
onesclonesclonesclon
esclonesnesclonesclonesclonesclo
nesclonesnesclonesclonesclonesnes

Txn	Description	Qty	Price
Sal	KINGSIZE	1	10.99
Sal	BOY WITH THE ARAB ST	1	12.99

| Amount Payable | | | 23.9 |

direct marketing

your flyer

said

'live n' direct

global warming

and **special**

effects

I responded

head first

in your kitchen

lewd mixer

of inhibition

keep me on

your mailing

list

Txn   Desc

Sal KINGSIZE

Sal BOY WITH

Amount Payab

Sunday Morning
once so sacred

now the stage

Sunday Morning
once so sacred
spirtually naked

now the stage
for the new religion
spirtually naked
pets a gerbil
is the wrong decision
new religion

macho man
wears his sunday best
a tattooed cliche
in a union jack
machovestan

get the kids a
happy meal
happy meal
that's the deal

make life plastic
make life plastic

save the god queen

god save the queen
that's the deal
that's the deal

god save the queen
god save the queen
god save the queen

Sunday Morning
once so sacred

now the stage
for the
spiritually naked

pets r us
is the
new religion

a gerbil
or hamster
is the decision

macho man
wears his sunday best
a tattooed cliche
in a union jack
vest

get the kids a

happy meal

make life plastic

that's the deal

god save the queen

what's that name they call it?

post something

yeah, post hypnotic suggestion

...like it's a week later

and you can still smell her perfume

on your skin

and in your clothes

but you're wearing different clothes

it's fucking strange

and you want her again

although when you left

you never exchanged phone numbers

just a polite kiss on the cheek

and a short walk

to st james's park underground

where somehow things seemed

strangely different

moved more slowly

quietly

and they reckon

that the slowdown is due

to a chemical reaction

in the brain

lasting for a couple of hours

sometimes days

after body and mind

have been seduced

by the stranger

who suddenly appeared

by your side at 1am

moment

and took a sip

from your cappuccino

emerging

with froth on her lips

and chocolate on her tongue

which suddenly

made its way towards me

then into

the magical night

where everything

seemed so perfect

locking fingers

floating

on a cushion of air

and I swear

I'll never forget

the incredible contours

of her body

in the half light of her bedroom

with blue curtains

which only goes to prove

that shakespeare

was right all along

with his theory

that the purest love

is definable

from the very first...

m o m e n t

I saw them

an entire army

standing patiently

in multi-coloured uniforms

on parade

in complete silence

most facing due east

but the occasional one

turned at a slight angle

in the morning sunlight

the generals

looking strong

and purposeful

the infantry

strategically placed

and ready for action

at a moment's notice

then suddenly

a massive explosion

as she invades

the bathroom

multi colour ed army

geoffrey concluded

that the pitch

was firm and true

but susceptable

to low bounce

at the nursery end...

st john's wood

...the conditions

were perfect

as play began

strange then

that five minutes

later

several damp patches

should appear

on a length

they say

there's prostitutes

at number nine'een

'saw one

in the cornershop

with 'oles in 'er jeans

seemed spaced

out

like she was on somethin'

buying condoms

and prawn cocktail crisps

'er top undone

'an scars on 'er wrist

prostitutes

me 'usband

saw one on tuesday night

standin' on the corner

in fishnet tights

he reckoned

it was karen's doorta

no one's seen 'er

since 'er step dad caught 'er

in the kitchen

with a needle

near

superdrug

the girl

with

the dreamy

eyes

walks by

her sweet

fragrance

hangs

in the air

in five

seconds

you've fallen

in love

she is

the very light

from above

superdrug

attitude

attitude

or wot?

ineptitude

and rot

the show

that never stops

for 5 million

have nots

a land

that time forgot

a plan

that lost the plot

the dustpan

camelot

prey to those

in smoky squats

the new age

primate

zero wage

and stagnates

lives with

anger and hate

will wage war

on the state

someday

attitude

or wot?

b&q Landscape

sunrise over essex
with it's b&q and burger king landscape
home of a growing population
of divorcees
evacuees of a social disease
called

~~'i want more out of life'~~

b

b&q

L

Landscape

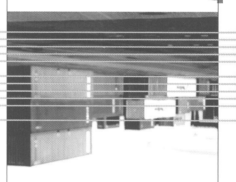

&andscape
b&q Landscape

sunshine over essex
on her upvc windows
on her semi detached
and council flats
on her car boot sale economy

~~and daytime gameshow~~

~~drudgery~~

sunset over essex
as the curtain closes
on an uneventful day of
videos and takeaways
and late night fights
in the subway lights
~~as southend lose~~
~~two nil~~

b & q

b&q Landscape
b&q La:

La

pe

andscape

but tonight
may the stars
shine down on essex
on her innocent children
and on her
homeless
who only know the moon
as a friend

ehs

dias

nrut

em

revo

yhcnuar
ettessac
lrig

l

yalp

eht

emas

htob

sedis

eastern

princess

asian

temptress

puts on

her

friday night

eyes

that

tantalise

and

hypnotise

e a s t e r n

but at

sunrise

she flies

p r i n c e s s

the

glittering

prize

she

lives

on

highs

defies

all ties

stiletto angel

in dry ice

heavenly shadow

from paradise

radiant vision

of desire

fragrant skin

sets hearts on fire

mother nature

so kind to some

stars shine on

her chosen ones

rythmic dancer

reigns supreme

mystic enchantress

eternal dream

nightclub girl

dream
face
your
place

d
ice
n
tice

chain
smoke
spray
coke

hot
wire
got
fire

play
fight
say
bite

cool
chic
lec
tric

x
cite
two
nite

b
cross
b
boss

b
course

n
force

'hot wire'

hi
lo
stop
go

lip
stic
real
slow

the emptiness

of the day

after

9am

I drink

from the cup

you drank

coffee from

last night

I taste

lip seal

I miss you

sitting

at the table

where we

sat last night

by candlelight

I miss you

I hold

the pillow

where you

laid your

head

I imagine you

on the bed

I miss you

you're amazing

PA

with

d

gree

does

IT

@

BT

lives

in

country

lane

showers

in

acid

rain

dances

flam

enco

drinks

kenco

on

saturdays

drives

nissan

small ads

seeks

man

to

shower

with

build

ivory

tower

with

drink

from

the

fountain

of

life

with

she

the

dreamer

seeks

eternal

subliminal...

small ads

ultra slim
and light

typical battery
talktime · very little

clocks and calculates

unlimited roaming

100 entries a year
(names and addresses ·
little or no memory)

limited callback

she is
'first in freedom'

similar offers
available from
participating outlets

precautions: you know the score